Celebrating What truly Matters

POWERS IRISH WHISKEY
SHORT STORY COLLECTION

VOLUME ONE

AN ANTHOLOGY OF SHORT STORIES BY VARIOUS AUTHORS

EDITOR

PATSEY MURPHY, THE IRISH TIMES

ILLUSTRATIONS

IAN McCAFFREY

WWW.STORYBOARDS.IE

COVER & BOOK DESIGN

MAEVE CHAPMAN, IRISH DISTILLERS PERNOD RICARD

ACKNOWLEDGEMENTS

A huge thank you to each individual author for their wonderful short stories, a creative generosity without which this collection would not have been possible.

A special thanks to Patsey Murphy for her invaluable contribution, whose practical advice and attention to detail have been crucial in bringing this project to fruition.

To Sheila O'Flanagan and the Irish Hospice Foundation for their ongoing support and generosity of spirit.

To all those involved in Celebrating What Truly Matters,
thank you.

THE IRISH TIMES
irishtimes.com

ISBN: 978-0-9570784-0-6

Printed in Ireland

THE IRISH HOSPICE FOUNDATION

Foreword

SHEILA O'FLANAGAN

Storytelling is in every Irish person's blood. We're good at it. We tell stories on buses, on trains, standing in queues, over a cup of tea or maybe something stronger. And sometimes we write them down, as over 3,000 people did for the Powers Irish Whiskey short story competition in the Irish Times this spring, embracing the theme of Celebrating What Truly Matters. That so many people took the time to write their story shows just how much the written word still means to us as a nation.

I've always loved the short story. I love its simplicity and how so much information is imparted to the reader in so few words. Short stories can pinpoint a major turning point, or reflect on a moment in time, give us pause for thought, or make us laugh. They allow us a glimpse into a character's life, drawing us in so that we are totally engrossed in the moment and totally lost in the story being told. We don't want it to end but we are satisfied when it does, acknowledging that the writer has done a good job, even as the tale resonates with us long after we've finished.

Short stories are often underrated precisely because they are short, but they require the skill of a master craftsman to accomplish what they need to. They require a light touch, a deftness of phrase and an economy of language that doesn't come easily. In a good short story, every word has its place, nothing is wasted, and there is no room for unnecessary diversions. Yet there is an enormous advantage for the short story writer over the novelist, in knowing that the finishing line is always close at hand. For me, as a writer, the short story is a quick fix of creativity, when I can lavish all my attention on one character and one dilemma and resolve it in a lot less time than it takes to write a novel.

However, there is a huge emotional challenge in writing a good short story, in seeing characters and situations develop in the single moment of the writer's choosing. And then there is the relief when it is done and shared and when other people understand the reason the story was written.

It is important to preserve our stories and to write them down. Which is why books like this are so wonderful. Filled with joy and sorrow, laughter and tears, every story will draw you in, and reward you for reading it. All of the writers deserve their selection in this collection, and it is uplifting to know that all of the proceeds from its sale go to the Irish Hospice Foundation.

Each short story is unique in itself and this is a unique book. It deserves its place in your heart and on your bookshelf.

Sheila O'Flanagan is the international number one best-selling author
of sixteen novels and three collections of short stories.
Her books have been translated into over twenty languages.

Powers Whiskey, one of the great Irish symbols of quality, authenticity and tradition is delighted to showcase some of Ireland's hidden and golden literary talent in Celebrating What Truly Matters: Powers Irish Whiskey Short Story Collection.

This anthology was inspired by a hugely popular campaign for Powers which ran in the 1980s based on conversations and short stories. A nugget of social history, the campaign was an extraordinarily successful one, not only because of its wonderful, heart-warming stories and charming illustrations, but because everything sat so easily with the brand. It was a perfect fit, quintessentially Powers. As a rich, round and full flavoured whiskey of exceptionally good taste and character, Powers featured in each of the campaign stories and continues to play a central role in this collection.

Penned by writers from across the country, this collection reflects on mellower moments in time and the warmth of relationships, family and friends. All proceeds will go towards supporting the Irish Hospice Foundation's range of programmes including the development of bereavement services, hospice services and development of palliative care in the community.

We would like to take this opportunity to thank each of the contributors for their creative efforts in Celebrating What Truly Matters, a selection box of uplifting stories that will live on in the inspirational work of the Irish Hospice Foundation.

ANNA MALMHAKE

CEO IRISH DISTILLERS PERNOD RICARD

Contents:

Going for Gold

MARIAD WHISKER, DUBLIN

The familiar turquoise table squatted between them on three copper legs. The years have been kinder to it than to Eileen. Gone was the elfin-faced beauty. A soft roundness filled out her cheeks and the substantial heft of her hips took Harry by surprise. This Eileen bore little resemblance to the skinny student who had sashayed past him in the college canteen, her lime-green velvet bell-bottoms and floaty voile blouse leaving little to his imagination.

Obama smoldered like a movie star on the television screen that sat atop a dated chrome drinks cabinet. His rousing words filled the awkward silence. Harry broke it.

"Great to see the oul' Trickeler fluttering away beside Old Glory."

"It's tricolour, Harry. I can't believe you're still calling it a trickeler.'

Harry laughed.

"Tricolour, trickeler? Green, white and gold, green, white and orange? What does it matter?"

"It's what the Tricolour means that matters, Harry."

Rolling her eyes Eileen heaved herself out of the armchair. Stomping into the kitchen she wished she'd not been wearing her tracksuit when he'd appeared out of the blue like that.

Harry thought back to the ferocious debates they used to have. Upstairs in the attic of this very same house, into the early hours with Van Morrison yearning away in the background. Her Da thumping the hall ceiling with a broomhandle.

"Have you no home of your own to go to, wee lad?"

Harry would quietly slope off. From her estate to his own estate, on the other side.

If it hadn't been for jet lag he wouldn't be sitting here in her living room, maundering on about the past. If he hadn't wandered down to the lobby on his second sleepless night and got that stack of newspapers from the concierge, he would never have spotted her name in the Death Notices. He would never have bought that newspaper in the first place.

MCNULTY – Late of Fruithill Park. Beloved husband of the late Bernie. Deeply regretted by his loving daughter Eileen and grandchildren, Josephine and Ciara.

His Eileen. And no mention of a husband.

She came back into the room and put a glass of juice on the table in front of him.

"Now Harry. That's what I call orange." Her playful smirk broadened into the infectious grin he remembered.

Leaning forward, he slid the glass of orange juice towards her side of the table. He turned towards the television. Eileen followed his gaze downwards, from Obama, to the bottle of Powers Whiskey on the top shelf of the drinks cabinet. Harry smiled.

"Whatever you're having yourself, Eileen. But you know what? I'm still going for the gold."

Without a Backward Glance

DEIRDRE MANNING, GALWAY

Mags turned in the direction of the voice that called her name. It took a second for recognition to dawn. He was older, greyer, but still heart-lurchingly, drop dead gorgeous.

"Chris," she said.

"You haven't changed a bit," he replied.

"I'd take that as a compliment, but if I looked this old twenty odd years ago it's no wonder you married someone else."

His once familiar laugh seemed to fill the airport as they walked towards the luggage carousel.

"I always think of you as the one that got away."

"That's a laugh!" she grinned. "You dumped me, without a backward glance."

God, it had really hurt at the time. He'd suddenly run off and married a woman who put significant cash into his fledgling wine business. Mags had lent him her life savings to buy his first van. She got her first credit card so that she could buy expensive clothes that were appropriate for the significant other of a wine merchant. It took her several years to recover financially after he left, and even longer for her heart to heal. Her life had revolved around him. At wine tastings she had watched the clients admire the meniscus, gaze at the legs, while eulogising the nose. She endured discussions about the fruity aftertaste or the element of cat's pee. She thought she was in her element. The memories made her wince.

"How is Louise?" she asked.

"We're divorced," he replied.

"But not before your business took off."

"You've been keeping tabs on me."

How smug, she thought, then she cursed as her unmistakably gaudy case came within reach, complete with the shocking pink scarf her daughter had tied onto the handle.

"Let me get that for you," he said swinging it off the carousel. "We must meet again. What's your mobile?" Noticing her hesitate, he handed her his card.

She grabbed her case awkwardly and lurched towards the arrivals hall. Brendan was there, anxiously scanning the crowd as if he half expected her to have missed the plane. His face lit up when he saw her. She knew that his face would light up again when he saw the bottle of Powers Gold Label she had bought in the duty free. And he'd smile as they shared a nightcap. He was dead easy to buy for, dead easy to be with. He took her case and her arm. She told him their daughter was no longer homesick in Paris because she had met an American student and was besotted.

Chris came into the arrivals hall just in time to see Mags leave with a tubby, balding man. As they reached the exit she threw a small white card in a bin and walked into the cold December night. Without a backward glance.

When Harry Met Madeleine

MARY ELIZABETH BURKE-KENNEDY, TIPPERARY

"I'm getting out of this house until you've calmed down."

"How can I calm down when every time I tidy something up you come and make a mess?"

"It's called living."

"You had a big breakfast. What are you doing eating scones and covering the counter with crumbs and jam?"

"It's lunchtime. They're not due for hours."

"I just want her first impression to be a good one."

"Her first impression of you will be that you're a raving lunatic."

A dangerous silence ensues, accompanied by angry swiping of the counter and flinging of cutlery into the drawer.

"All I'm trying to do is make the place right for our son and his girlfriend, who I suspect he wants to marry."

"In which case she will want to find herself in a family home, not a magazine supplement."

"Her parents have a chateau. She's used to style. She's French. She's used to rational behaviour. Look at those mucky shoes. I should put those damned things in the bin."

"Why don't you put me in the bin? That's what you'd like to do!"

The doorbell rings suddenly and Harry's voice calls, "Hello, you two. We're here. Anybody in?" And Harry opens the front door. In the kitchen, Maura and Joe are momentarily transfixed. Harry leads Madeleine into the kitchen and a flurry of "Come here to me" and hugs and kisses are unleashed on him. "You're looking great, so are you, great to see you, this is great."

And now Madeleine is presented. Small, thin, red-haired, she insists on three kisses "in the way of the South of France".

"I'm all for that," says Joe, "but if I didn't know you were French, I'd think you were Irish with that hair."

"In France we were Celts before we were French," she says.

"That accounts for her love of Irish whiskey," says Harry.

"Yes, Madame, I have for you the whiskey Harry says you like." Madeleine produces a bottle of Powers.

"Please, no Madame for me. I'm Maura."

"What do you say we have a small drop now," says Joe, "to celebrate. I was thinking all the time on the plane about tucking into one of Mum's scones."

"I have heard about Maura's scones."

"Let's break out. We'll have both," says Joe. "I'll get the plates and the glasses. You sit down, Mum. Relax. You too, Dad, let us feel at home."

While the scones are being buttered and the whiskey iced, Maura exhales.

"Good to hear you breathing again," says Joe.

"She's very nice, isn't she? "

"Harry's his father's son. Knows how to pick well."

"Sorry I got het up."

"You're grand, and by the way, take your curlers out."

Grand Night

HILARY FENNELL, DUBLIN

My father was standing outside the front door, staring at the full moon. As usual, he was pretending not to be waiting for me.

"Grand night," he nodded towards the moon as my suitcase wheels crunched towards him through the gravel.

"It is," I agreed, although I was dreading the task that lay ahead. We stood together silently for a while, heads turned towards the autumn night sky, until he picked up my case and, ignoring the wheels, carried it inside.

I followed his slightly stooped frame down the long, dark hall and into the kitchen at the back of the farmhouse. I could feel the old place welcoming me back, giving me courage. From her favourite spot beside the fire, our ageing collie Bertha greeted me by brushing her tail against the stone floor. I handed my father the bottle of Powers Gold Label I always brought him. He smiled his thanks and placed it on the dresser. We sat down at the wooden table in awkward silence.

"How was the traffic?" He folded his newspaper at the crossword.

"Not so bad, for a Friday," I ran my ringless fingers along the ridges in the tabletop, picking at the odd knot in the grain.

"You'll stay the weekend?"

My father watched my fidgeting and placed his pen on top of the paper.

"I will."

It was now or never, I had to tell him the reason for my visit. But I couldn't find the right words.

The carriage clock ticked. The low hum of the nine o'clock news came on the radio. Bertha snored in her sleep. My father was still looking at my hands. "The engagement's off, so?" he said matter-of-factly.

I stared at him, stunned at how he'd worked it out. "It wasn't Michael's fault, exactly, or mine..." I stammered. He walked over to the dresser, returning with the Powers and two of his best glasses. He opened the bottle, half filled each tumbler, and handed one to me.

"Before your mother met me there was another lad, you know." We drank as he let this news sink in.

"Broken hearted she was at first, when it ended. But she knew she deserved better."

I glanced over at my parents' black and white wedding photo on the mantelpiece. It radiated love.

"And you deserve better too," my father leant over and patted my hands gently. A soothing piano piece had come on the radio. The sweet smell of turf-smoke filled the air. The full moon shone in the window. "Grand night," my father took another sip of his whiskey. "It is," I agreed. Only this time, I really meant it.

Walking on Thin Air

MARGARET O'DOHERTY, DONEGAL

It had been a big mistake to pretend I was a hillwalker and now, as my feet and legs ached, I was paying for it. It had been so easy on the Internet. When PAT82 said hillwalking was a favourite hobby I replied, without thinking, that I did a bit too. I was just trying to keep the conversation going, as you do, then one lie led to another. Whenever he mentioned a walk he had been on I quickly flicked to a hillwalking website, and absorbed enough detail to suggest that I knew the terrain, so to speak.

It was harmless enough, I reasoned, not like being married and pretending to be single or anything like that. Similarly, I didn't think for a minute that he shared my interest in poetry even though he said he liked every poet I mentioned, no matter how obscure. Nothing is too obscure for Google, I figured. But of course, I should have come clean when he said he was coming to Donegal to walk Sliabh Laig with his group. It was close to my home but all I knew about Sliabh Laig was that it was high up, pleasant to look at, and not a good place for someone with vertigo. But now it was too late. I was in too deep. I had tapped in too many white lies.

Needless to say, I was nervous when we met for the first time on a Friday evening, although we had been chatting online almost every night for months. You assume everybody in an Internet chat room might be on the weird side, apart from yourself, of course. For starters, he didn't look at all like I had imagined, or gleaned from his photograph. He was, on inspection, much better looking. I'd been afraid we would have nothing to say to each other but we couldn't stop talking, speaking much faster than we ever could type. A dozen times I started to tell him that I never walked much further than the front door to the car, but each time it came out as how much I was looking forward to the walk.

Now, less than a mile into the ordeal, the rest of the group was already well ahead of us and my new boots were killing me. Blisters so soon, I marvelled, trying not to limp. We hadn't even left even ground.

"Do you want to take a rest?" he asked.

"Just for a minute," I said, sitting down on a rock.

"Here, a sip of Powers," he said, pouring out a measure from his hip flask.

"Thanks," I said, downing it gratefully. It slipped easily down my throat, and even reached my sore feet.

"You don't walk, do you?" he challenged.

"No," I admitted, shamefaced.

"Thank God for that," he said, sipping his own whiskey. "Neither do I."

Miss Trout

MAIREAD ROBERTS, CORK

Having grown up in a village shop in Kerry, it seemed natural to me to chat to whichever member of the Patel family happened to be serving me in the Earls Court Road Convenience Store. Uncles, cousins, brothers, I never worked out quite what the connections were. To be honest, these conversations had been entirely one-sided for nearly a year, until the morning I added the Racing Post to my Irish Times.

"You sure you want this Miss?"

"Oh yes, thank you, just for this week. Cheltenham's on."

"You know about horse racing?"

"Not a lot, my brother Kevin is a stable-lad in Paddy Maguire's yard, and one of the horses he exercises is running today in The Bumper and Kevin has great hopes for him. He loves Brown Trout, says the horse talks to him."

With this I was out the door and into the scrum of the Piccadilly Line. That evening I was back in the convenience store exploring the charms of the chilled cabinet, when for the second time that day, and only the second time in a year, a member of the Patel family addressed me:

"Miss, my uncle, he wants to speak to you, follow me please."

I was ushered past the Staff Only sign, across a yard, towards a doorway screened by a mass of swaying beaded strings. The beads parted and there in the semi-darkness sat a Buddha-like figure enthroned on a stack of beer crates, his smile causing most of his face to disappear behind his spectacles.

"Miss Trout, Miss Trout come, come, we must celebrate the winner of today's Bumper. He came from behind, surprised everybody, a great victory, 12-1, I tell you, a great victory."

My host reached behind a carton of crisps and brought forward a bottle of Powers Gold Label and two polystyrene cups. Tottering to his feet, Mr Patel half-filled the cups, and puffing out his not inconsiderable chest, he cleared his throat:

"A toast to Brown Trout, my new friend Miss Trout and a great start to the Cheltenham Festival. As Mr Obama would say: Yes we can! Is feidir linn!"

With this perfectly accented toast, Mr Patel sank back onto his crate throne and pointed me to the crate beside his. He then slipped a sharpened pencil from behind his ear and the Racing Post from under a cushion, "Sit, sit, my dear Miss Trout, you must take your time and enjoy your Irish whiskey. We have horses to pick for tomorrow, what would you be thinking of in the Gold Cup?

Another great Irish horse, I am guessing.

Jim'll Fix It

SALLY WINTERS, DUBLIN

Sadie opened the door of Toner's Pub and hesitantly stepped inside. Would she really meet her soul mate tonight? She sniggered at the phrase. A successful freelance project manager with a comfortable home in a vibrant part of Dublin, life was good, but, she had to admit, seriously lacking in lustre and love.

"JIM, 38, no ties, tall, dark, handsome, likes current affairs, politics, seeks attractive caring female for friendship, maybe more", read the advertisement in The Ticket. Replying on impulse, she thought no more about it until a text arrived some two weeks later: "Toner's snug at 7 on Thursday, Jim".

She was more used to giving orders than taking them, and had at first felt vaguely annoyed that this stranger assumed she would be there. However, she also secretly liked the idea of meeting a man with initiative, who would take the lead and not expect her to make all of the decisions. After all, she made enough of those every day in her working life.

On entering the snug, she saw a rather handsome, rugged, dark-haired man seated in the corner, engrossed in a newspaper.

"Hi, I'm Sadie," she said, uncertain what the protocol was for a blind date.

"Hi, I'm James," he said. "Can I get you a drink?"

"Yes, thank you, whatever you're having yourself," said Sadie, feeling ridiculously flustered.

"I'm drinking Powers Gold Label," he replied.

Sadie was not accustomed to drinking whiskey and immediately regretted not making her own choice, but it was too late. In no time at all, James was back from the bar with her drink.

"Here's to us," he said, raising his glass.

"Yes, to us," she responded, feeling unusually heady and somewhat mesmerised. She took a sip of whiskey and felt an unexpected sense of well being. Could this be a coup de foudre I see before me?

The conversation was so fluent and intriguing that Sadie was startled by the beep of her phone and resented the interruption. It was a text message. Glancing at her inbox, she read: "Hi Sadie, sorry I can't make tonight, let's meet another time. Jim."

She blanched, realising her mistake. Mortified, she decided to come clean, and started to sputter apologies for throwing herself upon an unsuspecting stranger.

"Really?" James laughed, as he got up to order two more whiskies. "Well isn't that a fine how do you do?"

Mother Superior

EVA PLAZEWSKA, DUBLIN

"What kind of fool makes Christmas pudding on Christmas Eve?" she mumbled to herself. Maggie had the currants, the sultanas, the candied peel and cherries glistening like sticky jewels in their little round tubs. She'd even remembered to get a can of stout. "Mixing bowl, mixing bowl…" she said out loud, as if one might magically appear out of thin air.

Mammy's recipe was written in a crabbed scrawl on the back of a torn envelope. "Could look it up online... but it wouldn't be the same. It would be cheating," she thought, stirring the sludgy mixture. It looked too brown. She began to panic. "I should give up now and order one in and Mammy will never know… If you can get, say, a Cambodian take-away at 3.30am on a Tuesday, someone, somewhere in New York must be able to deliver a traditional Christmas pudding…"

She poked her tongue out through her teeth and stared again at the recipe. Leave the mix sit, it ordered, although for how long it didn't say. She did the dishes to calm her nerves and gave the place a final once over before Mammy and her all-seeing, all-knowing eyes appeared.

The sudden knock at her apartment door made her jump.

"Mam, Dad! H-how did you get up here?" She wrestled the giant case from her dad's hands.

"What kind of welcome..." said Daddy.

“A nice young Chinese lad let us in,” said Mammy.

“Korean,” thought Maggie. They bustled inside, draping scarves and overcoats and duty free bags all over the floor and the sofa.

“You're quite high up,” said Daddy, gazing out the window at the city, his arm around Maggie's shoulder.“ You must be doing well for yourself, you've got a lift and everything.”

Then came the inevitable.

“What in heaven's name is that?” came Mammy's voice from the kitchenette.

Maggie's cheeks went red. “Eh, I was trying to make you a Christmas pudding.”

“ It's a bit late for that,” said Mammy, scooping up a spoonful of the mixture. “Not bad,” she said, while Maggie's mouth fell open. “Needs something though.”

“We got you this,” Daddy proffered the duty-free bag, oblivious to the pudding-based power struggle gathering momentum. Maggie began pulling open the bag and was just drawing out the bottle when her mother swooped.

"Perfect!” she cried, “A bit of Powers Gold Label will improve it no end.”

She unscrewed the top and sloshed a good measure into the solidifying pudding mixture.

“Now,” she said, standing back and admiring her handiwork, “it's good. I brought you one of my own Christmas puddings. Made it in September. It should be just right for eating by tomorrow.”

A Breath of Hot Air

PHILIP DAVISON, DUBLIN

Justin lurched from one crisis to another, ever willing to believe that he would be saved. His best friend, Robert, had no such belief, but had indeed saved Justin from ruin on many occasions. This new situation, however, threatened to undo them both. Justin's wife had left him, Robert's girlfriend wasn't returning his calls, and now their joint business venture was imploding. Robert's modest apartment, willed to him by his beloved uncle, was up for collateral and was about to be repossessed. These young men were in need of fellowship, mature guidance, and a pot of cash.

They decided to tap Larry, Justin's father, for a loan. Larry was a formidable self-made man, who stuck avidly to – and often repeated – the old adage "neither a borrower nor a lender be". Thus Justin made Robert do the asking, but warned: "Whatever happens don't go up with my father in his hot air balloon." Ballooning was apparently his father's dodgy new obsession and as a balloonist, he was uncharacteristically irresponsible.

To get to Larry, a person had to go through Justin's mother, an affable woman and a pragmatist. Fortunately for Robert, she had a soft spot for him. She invited him over, poured him a Powers Gold Label, and called her husband in from the field behind the house. Robert relaxed. This business meeting was going to be a breeze, he decided. Little did he know.

Larry shook his hand vigorously. "You want some advice, my wife tells me."

"Eh, yes…" replied Robert.

"Right, so. Why don't you come up in my balloon so that I can advise to you from a great height."

There was no way out. Up and away they went, crossing over lanes with high hedges and skimming a few treetops until they drifted clear over a farmhouse and a dangerous-looking church spire. Eventually they came to a bendy river Robert knew well from fishing expeditions. Larry brought the balloon down quite suddenly and dipped the bottom of the basket in the water. For a moment, they floated up stream.

"Now," he said, as they ascended again. "Advice…"

Robert took a deep breath and out came this feeble opener: "A little investment?"

"Ah. Haven't you heard, you should never go into business with your best friend."

"Too late."

Larry narrowed his eyes, and almost smiled.

"Balloon one to Mrs. P. Over."

Justin's mother was following the balloon's erratic course in her car. She lifted her shortwave radio. "Yes, Larry? Over."

"Tractor ahead. Take the next left. Cut across under us. Over."

"Thank you, darling."

Larry made a bags of the landing and got a bump on his head. Mrs. P tended to it. Robert got his cheque – for being loyal. It was time for another Powers.

His feet were still wet when he lifted the phone, and tried to ring his girlfriend once again. But he knew she'd find this latest episode more than a little far-fetched. He knew he might need to take her up in a balloon himself to convince her otherwise.

A Mother of All Rants

DOIREANN MARKHAM, ROSCOMMON

Ten minutes was an impressive rant, but not her longest. She once heckled me from the stand for a whole game after I took her son off during the first half of a league match. Tonight, the third such lecture this year, the topic was her son Paid's relegation to the bench the previous week, not mentioning, of course, Paid's inability to catch a cold, never mind a sliotar, and his pronounced aversion to running.

"You put in dire, friggin' Twomey," she screeched, "that tank must be thirty six if he's a day... It must be twenty years since I taught him, or tried my best to anyway. You of all people should believe in our Paid. T'was you that put the hurl in his hand and him only ten months old, amn't I right Peter?"

Jaysus, didn't I regret the day I gave him that hurl.

"Oh, you're right, six months he was, six months," her husband muttered, checking the time on his phone.

As she blustered on, my mind wandered to Murphy's pub and the whiskey I'd looked forward to all evening. My father's words resounded in my ears: "Family, friends, Murphy's open fire and a glass of Powers… any more is greed." My mind clouded over as I thought of the rest of the lads, nice and warm down there.

Having heard her call Twomey a useless lump, an amadán and, for some reason, a headless bullock, I cut across her, giving her the usual about how there was always next year and the high hopes we had for him etc. Then, in a sterner voice, I swore I'd ban her from all Junior B games for twenty, no, forty years if she came near me again about those sons of hers. Naturally, that didn't go down well and with eyes blazing she declared that I was "nothing but a fool that wouldn't know talent if it lap-danced for me, isn't that right Peter?"

"It most certainly is dear," he responded as they walked to the car.

I locked up and headed down to Murphy's where, around the fire, discussion raged regarding the best full-back line the Gaels had ever seen. Standing at the bar, I nodded at Peter and grumbled,.

"You'd want to get a friggin' muzzle for that wife of yours. Twenty minutes - twenty friggin' minutes – she went on, the wagon."

He ordered me a Powers and chortled heartily,

"Muzzle? Your sister? I'd like to see you try. You'd have more luck trying to make Paid run."

Small World

CLAUS CHRISTENSEN, WICKLOW

"Powers Gold," he said to the Chinese barman in an unmistakable Irish accent that caused her to notice him for the first time. "Of all the gin joints, in all the towns, in all the world, he walks into mine," she said by way of introduction, and he smiled when he picked up her Irish accent. Even Shanghai is a small town, he thought. He offered to buy her a drink and she said she'd have what he was having, only with ice. They chatted amicably and were glad for one another's company.

Outside, red fireworks crackled and hissed in the peculiar opaque sky that hangs over China's flagship city. "It must be fate that Mayo should come across Sligo in a city of twenty million on the eve of Chinese New Year," he said, half believing it himself.

It was late and the barman poured alcohol across the counter and lit it, sending flames spewing into the air like the breath of a dragon. The mutating throng, an international mix of expats and Chinese, were only too happy to chase it, knocking back unnaturally coloured shots of baijou served in test tubes.

This was not quite how either of them had expected Communist China to manifest itself. But, however it bared its teeth, not to mention its undergarments, they felt like they were watching the future unraveling.

"It's surreal. I feel like I've landed in Blade Runner," he said. "Do you?"

They could feel the excitement of the night mounting. The atmosphere was electric and the notion of time travel was suddenly credible. They thought that it might be similar to the hedonism of 1930s Shanghai before the Cultural Revolution – or to Dublin five years ago, they muttered. Across the river from the rooftop bar, the futuristic high rise skyline was flashing neon, and the space age Oriental Pearl TV Tower twinkled like a million rubies.

"Twenty years ago none of this existed. Shanghai is proof that a city can reinvent itself," she said.

"Now if we could only just bottle that notion and bring it home it might be worth importing," he added.

"You know the Shanghainese are developing a taste for whiskey," she said casually, but quickly warmed to her theme. "Maybe we should think about going into business. Export Irish whiskey, import Shanghainese chutzpah," and they laughed at the mangled phrase.

If only.

They decided to sleep on it.

The Shot

PAUL HANDRICK, WEXFORD

She sat huddled against the heather. Still. Watching. Downwind, always downwind. She scanned the purple expanse before her as far as the ridge. She waited. Her eyes watered, stung by the wind which raced from the top and embraced every crevice with its icy kiss; the jagged rock in front of her only occasionally providing shelter. One shot. That was all she needed. One shot and she could leave. Waiting. Anticipating the shot.

Waiting. She had found her position early and now the sun was at her back, low, ready to leave her to the night. One hour she reckoned at most and she must leave. Cold. She slipped her right hand from the glove into her breast pocket and retrieved a small flask. Her fathers. Now hers. She removed the top and raised it to her lips, her eyes all the while dancing around the landscape. A moment. Then the warmth of the whiskey comforting her. Radiating. She missed him. She was very much her father's daughter. Even down to his drink – Powers. Straight.

She remembered him by the fire, newspaper in hand, smiling at something he had just read. His glass balanced on the arm of the chair, precariously. The memory and the whiskey warmed her and she became lost in her thoughts, staying far, far longer than she had intended. Darkness spread. A low moon was falling off the mountain.

Then it appeared. Her quarry. Instinctively she reached forward. Leant in to take the shot. Her breath held. She focused. Just one shot. She stopped. Slowly eased back. This time there would be no shot. Before her stood the

stag silhouetted perfectly by the moon. Ancient. Timeless. She sat and watched this proud beast, a relic of a different earth, surveying his land and she felt like an intruder. There would be no shot.

She realised she was still holding her breath. She exhaled. The stag turned his head toward her and stared. She held his gaze, mesmerised. How many of his kind had fallen to man at this sort of moment, she wondered. In a moment, he turned and was gone. She stayed still for a long time, and then packed away her camera and found her torch to leave. The long wait had been worth it. She patted her breast pocket. "Thanks, Dad."

Twist of Fate

BRID CAHILL, LONGFORD

Cassidy's head bobbed up and down in the water as I frantically untied the rib at the stern of the cruiser. I made a dash with flailing paddles but, before I could reach him, he had disappeared. The wind kept rising. The choppiness on the lake made it impossible to mark where he went down, and when he resurfaced, I was well down-wind of him. Another dash - but a similar result.

He appeared one more time. Holding the rib against the wind I scanned the heaving water. Glimpsing the top of his head I pulled on the paddles straining every muscle but, caught in a trough, the rib sprang up with the curve of a wave, flicked over and capsized. Never much of a swimmer I grabbed at the upturned rib and levered my body onto it, face down, my fingers clawing the pontoons. Could I hold on as we drifted with the on-shore wind?

My mind now focused upon my own survival. An hour earlier I had set out alone to take my cruiser Tranquility to Dromod harbour. Without warning, the engine had stalled right in the middle of Lough Boderg. After a few frenzied attempts to restart it, I glanced at the dials and was amazed to see the fuel gauge showing empty despite having recently filled the tank. Shocked, I rushed out in the hope of seeing and hailing another boat. My feet slipped on the deck and I stumbled to my knees. The instant I fell, a body brushed the back of my head, then tumbled over me down into the water.

Now, face down on the capsized rib, I scarcely knew what had happened. Cassidy must have stowed away on Tranquility. But why? I knew him just to see. He had come into the town a year before, bought a grand house and car and exhibited a certain air of affluence. I had heard that he was paying some attention to my wife but dismissed the rumour as mischief. Obviously, he had planned something, but why did he jump overboard?

Another nasty chop almost swept me off the rib. In that moment I realised it was I who was meant to go over the deck-rail. The stumble had saved my life. What then? Who syphoned off the fuel from the locked-in tank? Was she in on this? It was this last question that brought my face up off the rib. I had survived and this, despite everything, was apparently my lucky day.

Tranquility was aground on the shore some thirty metres away. I waded through the reeds and climbed on board. Blissful reunion. A shaft of light fell on a bottle of Powers Gold Label, and with it, the promise of revival. But a torrent of questions remained. Where, I needed to know, was my wife? Was she somewhere, watching? Had she witnessed this fatal undoing?

This is the Life

KAY McLOUGHLIN, WATERFORD

The children waved off to school, her backpack ready in the hall, she makes a phone call while she fills the flask: "Meet you in fifteen minutes, the tide is full at ten o'clock." The chaos of breakfast left behind in the kitchen, they meet at the corner and walk briskly out the coast road under a clear blue sky.

The two friends talk easily and freely as they walk, about their children, their husbands, their work, what they are reading, what they will cook for dinner.

"That's an easterly wind, it will be cold."

"We'll be grand, we'll find a sheltered spot."

The narrow lane to the cove is brimming with yellow gorse, the scent of it and the white hawthorn sweet in their nostrils. There are clumps of bluebells and wild garlic in the ditch, everything bursting with the promise of brighter days ahead. The sparkling water opens up before them; they undress and run into the sea, the cold shock overwhelming. They cannot suppress their shouts and yelps. The ice cold water engulfs them, makes them feel alert, alive, rejuvenated. An easterly breeze sweeps across the waves, their skin stings from cold of it. They turn their faces to the sun, their arms and legs thrashing, laughing. Heart-stopping but undiluted happiness! She looks to the heavens, feels so alive and grateful for this moment, and shouts her mother's mantra: "Only dust if you must!"

They run to their towels, their feet numb now, not feeling the pebbles that hurt them before. They encase themselves in hoodies and struggle with socks and scarves and finally sit on the rug with their backs against the warm cliff, the unmistakeable smell of egg sandwiches oddly comforting as the tinfoil is peeled open.

The flask is opened.

“Did you bring it?”

“I did of course.”

A small bottle of Powers Gold Label whiskey is pulled triumphantly out of the backpack. Still shivering, they pour it into their mugs and sip it slowly, savouring the heat. Their lips begin to turn a lighter shade of blue.

“Sure isn’t the swim worth it when you can feel this great afterwards?” They laugh again, and swear they’ve got to do this more often.

The Boy on the Blue Bicycle

GILLIAN GALLIE, KILDARE

The balcony was a good place to think, the lapping of the waves and the cheerful calls of the stallholders setting up for the evening market on the pavement below had become familiar and comforting sounds. Woks were heating up and soon faint aromas of fragrant Thai cooking wafted on the warm breeze. This had been a good move, I thought, though not an easy one. I had found a great job and our accommodation was situated at the better end of Pattaya, well away from the seedy underbelly of bars and strip clubs. My wife, Niamh, had found it more difficult to settle in Thailand, but was slowly coming around, getting to know people and the language by teaching English and volunteering at a nearby orphanage. She had become especially fond of Annan, a strong streetwise boy of twelve, with haunted eyes that had no doubt seen too much, too young. He had arrived at the orphanage on his one material possession of any consequence, a battered blue bicycle. He stayed a month and then left as abruptly as he had arrived, taking nothing but his bike. Niamh tried every channel to find or even trace him, but it was proving impossible.

I could see a tall blonde woman striding along the road towards the apartment; it was Niamh, she had a spring in her step, maybe there was some news. I poured a measure from our stash of Powers into two glasses as she ran up the steps, breathless, and pressed a glass into her hand.

"Annan came back on his blue bicycle," she said. "He had a skinny six-year-old girl on the crossbar. He couldn't understand what all the fuss was about, saying that he had only gone to fetch his sister."

"Where did he go?" I asked.

"To Bangkok," she replied. "Can you believe it?"

"But that's about 150 kilometres away," I exclaimed.

"He had no money so he cycled all the way there and back, relying on his street skills to survive."

We raised our glasses, and thought, once again, about how easy our own lives had been.

"To the power of human spirit," I said.

She took a sip, savouring the familiar taste. "And to the bravery and resilience of children."

"Does she look like him?" I asked.

"Yeah," she said quietly. "She has his eyes. And she never takes her eyes off him."

The Usual

NOLLAIG ROWAN, DUBLIN

I balanced a plastic bag of notes on the carrier while I unlocked my bike. Rain splashed on the back of my neck, trickling inside my cardigan. Torrential showers in May! All I wanted was to be home and warm, away from Trinity Library where I'd spent so many hours in the past four years. The wind whipped up and my bag tumbled, sheets scattering to the corners of Front Square. Disgruntled but sympathetic fellow students returned them to me and skulked away.

"Damn… where're the French notes?" I said to no one in particular.

"What's that Niamh?" said a familiar voice. I looked up. He handed me a clutch of soggy pages.

"Shane!"

I didn't need this. Not now, not in the middle of my Finals. I hadn't seen Shane since we split up, over a year ago, when he went to Berlin.

"You look frozen. C'mon and I'll buy you…" he said.

"No I have to…"

"Just one. In The Pav."

"The usual," Shane said to the barman who knew us.

"Not for me… I have to study. Get me a water…" I said, testily, though Shane was always good at knowing what I really wanted. He placed two

Powers in front of us and a sparkling water on the side.

“So,” he said relaxing, long time, eh?”

I didn’t want this conversation. I had moved on. He took a long slow sip of the whiskey and unwillingly caught its warm aroma on his breath, despite the respectable distance between us.

“So?” he said again.

“So, you’re back,” I said. “I’m at exams and …” The word “exams” always made me nervous. I picked up the whiskey and swirled it around in the glass before allowing the taste to explode in my mouth. I had felt nothing like this since… well, since before Shane went away. He moved closer. We drank silently, reflectively.

“When’s your last exam?” he said.

“Tuesday. Finishes at six.”

Unlocking my bike in Front Square on Tuesday evening, I felt a hand on my shoulder.

“How’d it go?” Shane said.

Not too bad… Good in fact! Yeah,” I said, feeling light and frivolous. I expected him to suggest “the usual” in The Pav. Instead he leaned towards me, his light stubble brushing against my cheek and whispered “I want to give you a baby.”

I lurched away from him, dropping my bike on the cobblestones and tripping over my satchel. Passing students stared at me and frowned at him. He bent to help me.

“A Baby Powers,” he laughed, taking two miniature bottles from his denim jacket. “Let’s sit on the grass. Isn’t it great you’re finished and have your exams behind you?”

Into the Storm

EMMET KELLY, DUBLIN

Drenched, I stood on the high cliff looking across the bay towards Boffin Island and watched for the tiny white boat that contained my father. Huge sea swells made him disappear until we were sure he was lost, but then a glint would appear again through the brackish gloom. Was his boat the right way up? It was impossible to tell. Towards Cleggan, I could see a funereal gathering of locals at the pier wall staring out into the storm. They knew that when the west wind raged, the sea was utterly ruthless. Terrified, we could only keep watch.

A fitness fanatic, Dad always pushed it. Swimming oceans. Racing trains. Vaulting mountains. Strolling continents. He'd arm wrestle an elephant if he could find one. This time my Dad, known locally as Superman, was now sitting in a pathetic piece of plastic surrounded by walls of water the height of Nepalese mountain ranges. They could accidentally swallow him up in a single gulp. He yanked his flimsy oars at ten-ton waves that bounced him toward razor-sharp rocks and cliffs and away from the safe harbour that was my mother, Cleggan and me. "I'll row from Cleggan to Boffin and back again," he'd said. What was he thinking?

The noon sky darkened. The sea didn't care. It could trade a man's life for the price of a fish; could isolate an island for months leaving the inhabitants to starve; could ruin our lives without a moment's hesitation.

As Dad's boat appeared ever closer, the fishermen got jittery. The maniac might just make it! they calculated among themselves. A small red trawler

went a short distance to meet him, though of course he protested that as he'd gotten this far, he'd go the full distance. Jubilant, he was carried shoulder high to the Pier Bar where several brimming glasses of hot Powers Gold Label were delivered to jump-start his rigid, frozen body and dissolve the salt that caked the words in his throat.

The celebrations that night were legendary, and long into the morning happy reels from his old violin carried up the mountainside and through my open bedroom window. Superman may have rowed from Cleggan to Boffin and back again in a hurricane, but more importantly, my dad was alive. What is it that drives people to break records and conquer new frontiers? Well, whatever it is, there's no stopping them.

The Kiss

ALEXANDRA BLACK, LOUTH

I'll always remember that night, that summer. As the sun sank into the sea, we lounged in the sunken armchairs at your parents' house, its foundations just meeting the cusp of the beach. You were just eighteen, somewhere in the haze between adolescence and manhood. You called all your friends, and they called theirs. Soon the house was filled with bodies, all wishing to see out the end of our first, intrepid, newly independent summer in style. Minutes and hours meshed into laughter and music, rhythm and beat. Then, you took me in one hand, and that exotic old bottle in the other. Powers Gold Label from your father's collection. Our fingers entwined, you led me out to the water, where we stood letting our toes melt into the wet sand. We took a few eye-watering sips from the bottle, allowing more than a few slight brushes of skin between each offering. We stood separated by three feet of salty night air and our own youthful anxiety.

The sea lapped around our ankles, filling the seemingly endless silence between us. We were just eighteen. Your hand met mine, your fingertips grazing my palm. I replied with two shuffled steps in the water to find you, to let my mouth meet yours as we finally embraced. In that moment we were alive with the insatiable hunger of our youth, with only the stars to bear witness. I am older now. You are, too. We lead separate lives in separate worlds. But, with just one sip from a dusty old bottle of Powers I can be with you again, standing in the water, just eighteen.

Viva La Stampa

JOCIE McEVOY, LOUTH

As she boarded the coach on the first day of her annual holiday, she felt that old familiar buzz of excitement. Luckily her favourite seat was vacant.

"Perhaps you would like the window seat?" asked the gentleman in the aisle, letting her slip in to the inside seat. She smiled her thanks, looking into a pair of mild blue eyes.

"Mosley" he said introducing himself. "T.J. Mosley." Everyone knew her as Little Audrey.

The following morning they shared a breakfast table. After that it seemed quite natural that they would take the same tours, visit the local stalls and admire the same sights together.

Day five was spent at the seaside. Little Audrey wore her new sundress and her precious sapphire pendant on a fine gold chain. Mr Mosley was especially gallant: "My dear I will be taken for your father," and "that lovely jewel brings out the colour of your eyes." Later they sat wriggling their toes in the warm sand, licking ice cream cones and paddling in the sea.

The following morning, however, Mr. Mosely was missing for breakfast. And for lunch. It wasn't until that evening that he returned in a state of great excitement. In a conspiratorial way he drew close to her and whispered "I'm a philatelist, and today I got the prize of all prizes. A Penny Black."

His eyes shone, and his hands trembled, as from an inside pocket he reverently removed a leather pouch containing a flat glass case. Reposing inside was the little stamp. "In mint condition," he said. Then, before tucking it away again "Very valuable."

As they said goodbye at the airport and smiled at each other fondly, in one of those spontaneous gestures Mr Mosley took Little Audrey's face in his hands and said "You brought a lot of joy into my life" and gave her a chaste kiss on the forehead. "Goodbye my dear."

Little Audrey hugged him, and then turning, ran up the steps to the plane.

Later as she put on the kettle in her modest home, her hand automatically felt – as it so often did – for her pendant. Missing. Impossible.

"Oh my God," then "Mr Mosley!" For a moment her eyes filled with tears as she remembered his parting gesture at the airport. But then the humour of it all struck her and she collapsed laughing in a chair. "Time to celebrate what really matters," she said, as she drew a leather pouch with its little glass case from her bag. And taking out her bottle of Powers Gold Label she raised her glass in a toast. "To you Mr Mosley," and looking at her nimble little hands thought it wasn't for nothing she was called Little Audrey.

Hit and Miss

HELENA DORAN, DUBLIN

Jim shifted uncomfortably, running his finger uneasily around the inner circle of his collar. He smiled companionably at his neighbours, and took a sip of his pink champagne. Bubbly they called it – he could see why. He was partial to a bit more depth. As he watched James toast his new baby girl, pride and sadness swelled within. His son had achieved more than any father could wish, but at a cost. Their old closeness felt somehow diminished; distance and life's demands crowding it out.

Anna, his daughter-in-law, clasped baby Emily tight. A beautiful baby, just like her mother.

Jim walked across the lawn, remarkably green and dense, breathing in the freshness. Anna must have been out with the nail scissors, he thought. It was perfect. The borders, immaculately disordered, fooled no-one. Every leaf and stem had been meticulously placed. Meticulous, that was the word. It summed Anna up. From the studied casualness of the garden, to the appropriately subdued music, the immaculate house, the baby pink balloons and flowers. Everything just so. How unlike he and Jean! Hit and miss, that was their style.

A pang of longing for his wife swept over him. Jean would have adored the fuss and ceremony of today and delighted in having a grandchild. And she would have chided him for being so critical. Jim suddenly remembered how Anna had gone to the hospice and modeled her wedding dress for Jean, who died not long before the wedding. Such kindness, he thought, wondering why he had been so judgmental all this time. Misplaced grief, he supposed, vowing to see more of them.

He turned and, pretending to admire some alliums, wiped his eyes with his handkerchief. Anna and James caught his eye. He was beckoned towards the house and dutifully followed them inside. "Just putting Emily down for a nap Jim," whispered Anna. "You take her."

Gingerly, and with an encouraging nod from James, he took the sleeping baby in his arms as they walked, single file, to the nursery. Baby pink and not a garment astray, naturally.

He placed her gently in the basket and turned at a touch on his shoulder. James stood, hand outstretched, offering him a tumbler of whiskey, while Anna continued pouring three more from the bottle of Powers Gold Label on the mantelpiece. Jim looked, puzzled, at the glass beside the photo of him, Jean and infant James. Then he looked at Anna, who with tears in her eyes, raised her glass.

"Emily Jean, may you grow to be as special as your Gran," she said.

Jim couldn't speak. But as they stood watching the baby sleep, words weren't necessary. Not necessary at all.

A Bend in the Road

PATSY J MURPHY, GALWAY

Maeve climbed out of the wrecked car and kicked its dented side. She had bruised her shoulder but otherwise was unhurt. She climbed up from the ditch and looked up and down the winding country road. Birds were beginning to settle for the night croaking their dusk song; the May thorn was turning to ghostly lace patterns on the hedges around her. No light shone on any welcoming home. She took out her damp hanky and sniffed into it. She had been crying when she hit the ditch. Mark had dumped her; he'd met someone else. An American doing a post-grad on Yeats. Mark had always been cutting about her domestic science diploma, and her driving.

She had fled from the city, and she would not have crashed if it weren't for Mark's treachery, she told herself. Visibility weakened by tears. No fiancé, no job. It was the emigrant ship for her, she thought, as she trudged up the road.

She jumped when a battered old car stopped beside her. A solid looking man of about forty leaned out of the window.

"Is that your car back there?"

"It is," she said shortly.

"The local garage is closed for the night," he said. Maeve scuffed the ground.

"You'd better come with me."

"Where to?" Maeve glared at him.

"Just up the road." A black and white collie stuck her head out the window. Murderers don't have collies, thought Maeve irrationally, and climbed in. The dog jumped on her lap and settled down.

"What happened to you?"

"I didn't see the turn. I was thinking of something else."

"Aye, it's a bad turn. You're not the first."

They rounded a corner and she saw a long low building. Light spilled out onto the road and shone on the sea below.

"Come in," he said, "you look half starved." Three old men sat by a turf fire playing cards.

"You're back so, Hugh," said one.

"I am," said her driver, and moved behind the bar.

"This'll warm you up." He reached up and poured a generous glug of Powers into a glass. Maeve took a sip and instantly felt a bit more cheerful.

"It's a nice pub," she said politely.

"Oh, it's quiet now, but we get a lot of tourists in the summer. My cousin was going to do tea and sandwiches this season for families on the beach. She's moving to Dublin, getting married, so I don't know now." Maeve raised her glass and sipped slowly. Then she smiled at him.

"I can make a great whiskey cake," she said.

Tall Tales

KAREN MAYE, DUBLIN

I was beginning to doubt the old adage that a bad day's fishing beats a good day working. It had not been a good day. We were in the boat on the far side of the lake when I realised I hadn't charged the battery in the fish finder. Jim, already annoyed at the absence of any new entries in his fishing log, left me under no illusion as to what he thought of me – though when he realised he had left my favourite box of flies in the hotel, I returned the sentiment. These were supposed to be glorious stolen days from work but when even warm sunshine became irritating, we called it a day.

Neither of us spoke as we hauled all the fishing gear up the road to the hotel. It took the sight of the Powers sign outside Keogh's pub to kick-start the conversation.

"Do you fancy dropping in for a quick Powers?" I asked him, answering my own question by quickening my step.

The barman greeted us with a "Well lads!" as we walked in. "Two Powers, please" was our reply, as we settled ourselves at the bar. This was my kind of pub. There were fine specimens of fish proudly displayed in dusty glass cases on the walls, the evening sun cast a warm golden glow over everyone, and an elderly man sitting quietly at the end of the bar raised his glass in response to ours. The most impressive fish on the wall was a 16lb brown trout caught on the fly by Peader Maye, April 3th, 1956. Now that would be a catch to talk about.

"That's some trout," I said to the barman.

"The largest ever caught on the lake," he replied.

Jim turned to look at it. "Sure I've caught tuna twice that size," he said, before proceeding to regale the group at the table next to us with his famous story of the tuna. My irritation with him returned. 30lbs?

"Well that's something," said the barman. He then turned to the elderly man.

"Well Peader, that's your record broken! Did you ever come close to catching anything that big?"

Realisation dawned on Jim and his cheeks instantly turned bright red. Peader chuckled.

"No," he said, taking a sip of his Powers and returning his gaze to his newspaper. "When I was fishing the fish never got the chance to grow that big." The bar erupted with laughter and much back-slapping of Peader.

Jim did the only thing he could do and ordered a round of Powers for the house. I turned my face smiling into the evening light and knew that tomorrow I would walk down to the lake carrying only my fly rod and my box of favourite flies tucked safely in my pocket.

Seize the Accordian

MICHEAL O'RAGHAILLAIGH, CAVAN

"Howaya doin'?" This is Sergeant Armstrong O'Raghaillaigh of the P.S.N.I. looking for help or at least not hindrance. Séan De Courcy from Swad currently residing in the Grantham Pease Nursing Home is holding a nurse hostage in his en-suite with his button accordion. He is demanding a minibus with safe passage to Swad. At present we are placating him with warm Powers Gold Label and ginger nut biscuits, but he could play at any moment. He has two tunes but some believe it's the same piece played slower – hard to tell. We could call in the crack team of the Mountain Road Pipe Band but things being as they are, John Kelly the banjo player from Enniskillen is on standby with Carrickfergus.

"A volunteer offer from the Ballinamallard Fifes and Drums was declined as it could cause a sectarian riot like last year, when it took days to clear the corridor of tangled up Zimmer frames. We thought the catering staff were attempting to lure him out with the smell of bacon and cabbage but were informed that in view of the situation the kitchen had been closed and this was the usual aroma of the place; and Séan is a fish man anyway. A hunting friend of Séan's said to give him a shotgun instead, as he had never hit anything before, just it would look so bad in the inquiry.

"All one hundred and fifty eight detainees, two nurses and twenty management staff are unable to pass his door to get out the main door; the emergency doors won't work, in fact on inspection they were found to be sheets of framed plywood nailed to the wall. On complaint, the deputy assistant manager emailed from Barbados informing us that they were above specification as said sheets were veneered in mahogany.

“Constable Iris Blossom offered to exchange places with the hostage but Séan said his taste in uniforms was specific. Constables Blossom, Andy Mann and Seymour Legg are conducting negotiations from the room adjoining the en-suite, they must be commended for their courage; it has taken its toll of course with Blossom’s blouse being torn (an unexpected pleasure for the onlookers) and poor Legg appears to be walking with a limp.

“As I was writing his parish priest said mass over the P.A. system and while Séan had his nap during the sermon, twenty paratroopers armed with fixed bayonets Morris-danced into the room where hand to hand fighting ensued, with Séan being overcome and the accordion bayoneted. A more serious result has been averted but I ask for more diligent searches to be carried out in the future and can’t help but wonder – what if he had been a Sean Nós singer?”

The Girl with the Pink Lipstick

DAVID O'NEILL, WICKLOW

What was I thinking coming back to this town after all these years; did I imagine I was going to find something I didn't even know I was looking for? Shaking my head I got up, said goodbye to Billy, and headed for the door, but as I opened it, I stood aside to let a young woman enter. She stopped in front of me and turned.

"Would you have a light?" she asked.

I was mesmerised by her beauty; she had long, thick fair hair and her eyes were like the Mediterranean compressed into marbles. But it was her smile that struck me and I think she was aware of her allure because she had painted her lips a dusky pink. If I spoke from my heart I would say "I want to kiss you", but of course no one speaks from the heart.

"I don't smoke," I muttered instead, and she turned to go. "But, em, could I buy you a drink?" I asked, banging my knee on the door frame. My timing was, as usual, just a tad off the mark.

But she turned back. "You've got one chance, then," she smiled. "Impress me."

My mind raced as we walked to the bar, the challenge of "one chance" sounding more like a threat than a dare. Billy was surprised to see me back, but summed me up the minute he saw her."What can I get you?" he asked, eyebrows aloft.

I was aware of her looking at me and panic began to rise in my chest as I peered behind the bar. Then I saw the bottle and took a deep breath.

"Two Powers Gold Label, straight up," I said, with a stab at bravado.

Billy obliged. She gently took the glass, tapped it with her long red finger nails, and took in the subtle aroma. We watched, she sipped. Billy and I stared at her as she replaced her glass on the bar.

"I don't smoke either," she turned to me, smiling.

Saving the Hay

SHEELAGH MOONEY, KILDARE

The Massey Ferguson moved slowly and deliberately between the deep-rutted grooves in the field, and when it reached the gate, shuddered to a halt as the passengers sitting perilously on top of the unsteady bales of hay on the trailer flattened themselves down. A cheer rose up as they narrowly cleared the overhanging trees and the tractor made its way slowly onto the roadway. My father smiled easily as he pulled on his pipe and the throttle simultaneously, throwing the laughing crew backwards onto the load. With a synchronised turn of heads they surveyed the empty fields from which they had come, the little ones with something of regret and the adults with a sigh of contentment at a job well done.

The gods had smiled on them this summer and if there had been any complaints they were few and restricted to the difficulty of working in welcome, but unusual heat. The tractor and trailer trundled along the windy, narrow road pulling in occasionally to let the odd car go by, only to be greeted with much horn-blowing and mock fist-waving in the air.

Finally, the tractor made its last sweeping manoeuvre into the haggard and across to the barn. My father began reversing over the cobblestoned yard to ensure that the trailer was aligned with the tidy stacks of bales already in the barn when the ropes began to loosen. In seconds, the high load began to tumble and bales were flying everywhere. As a six-year-old I watched as neighbours and relations took flight. Then I too was suddenly catapulted high in the air as my Uncle Packie grabbed the back of my t-shirt and we

parachuted over the edge to safety below. There were scrapes and bruises but no bones broken.

These were quiet men not given to over-dramatising events and nothing much was said other than a mild debate as to how to get the fallen bales into the barn without losing too much time. Finally the job done, a half dozen or so of Baby Powers were produced from the tractor and dispensed to the older ones who liked a drop; whether to celebrate the end of the hay-making season or to recover from the near mishap, I'll never know. Now I simply remember the lightness of their step and laughter as they threw back the whiskey and made their way across the yard and in through the kitchen door for the high tea that awaited them.

The Calm Before the Storm

ROBERT CAREY, DUBLIN

The door to the front room of our terraced house in Strandville Avenue was generally kept locked. It was opened for piano practice and very special occasions. The fire was rarely lit, the exception being Christmas.

In 1954 I was nine years old. It was the fabled time of the door left "on the lean" and getting messages "on the bill" in the Bayview Stores on the Strand. Our days were punctuated by the Eight Penny rush in the Strand Cinema, regular Saturday confessions in William Street, and the Dandy and the Beano on Tuesdays and Thursdays. Every evening, when Dad came back from Cusacks, he had a Baby Powers bottle tucked away in his jacket pocket. Himself and Mam would wind down the day before the dying fire in the kitchen with a comfortable sup each.

That year, my mother decided that the front room would be opened and the sitting room fire lit on December 8th, to celebrate the unveiling of a new carpet – a rare event. We would bring up the radio, play some music on the piano, sing a few songs and dine by firelight. Mindful of the new carpet, my mother insisted that every precious square inch be covered in newspapers to protect the pile from errant crumbs and worse. Luckily, we had been inundated with free copies of the newly published Evening Press, so there was no shortage of paper.

As we entered, the fire, lit earlier that day, crackled and fizzed in the hearth. And there, on top of the piano, surrounded by four small glasses, was no Baby, but a large bottle of Powers, gleaming in the firelight. Mam, Dad,

Paddy and Auntie Bee raised a toast and my brother Tom and myself overdosed on American cream soda. The newspapers were cast aside and old songs were sung and too soon it was time for bed for the smaller members of the family. As we fell asleep, we could hear the distant voices of the adults putting the world to rights, to the clinking of four small glasses.

That night, the Tolka River burst its banks, the Railway Bridge at East Wall Road collapsed, and Mam's beautiful carpet was buried under two feet of muddy river water. As Dad carried me on his shoulders out of the house, I looked behind me. The last thing I saw was his precious bottle of whiskey, floating down the hall and heading for the scullery.

Skipper and First Mate

CAROLE GURNETT, LIMERICK

It was all my bright idea. Borrow a cabin cruiser from a pal's dad, tootle around the bays and inlets of West Cork, a little sunbathing, a little eating, with evenings spent alfresco, sipping whiskey sodas. My girlfriend, Paula, petrified of water more than a foot deep, was wary.

"Don't worry", I said. "I'll look after you."

The cabin cruiser turned out to be a tub; that particular July was visited by monsoon-like weather conditions; and I failed miserably in the nautical skills department.

We had motored out in calm waters but as we neared Mizen, the wind picked up, the sea heaved and a rogue current drew us out further than was comfortable. The boat tossed. Paula sat astern, clinging to the railings to anchor herself against the roll of the vessel. Her face was a comic book shade of greenish white.

Pretending it was all good fun, I laughed into the wind and rain. Conditions worsened. I couldn't see land anymore because of the swell. Once the waves reached 12ft, I dropped the pretence.

"We're going to die," I shouted over my shoulder.

Every time we crashed down into a trough, the wheel was yanked out of my hand and began to spin alarmingly. Then something grabbed my ankle. It felt like the tentacle of a monstrous octopus trying to sweep me into the ocean. I yelled and lashed out only to find it was Paula. She had crawled across the floor and was using me to pull herself up.

"Brian, let me help," she shouted, regaining her balance. She gripped the wheel and between us we kept the boat on a steady course, rounded the point and found sanctuary in Dunmanus Bay.

When we moored, Paula had to prise my hands off the wheel. She took me downstairs to the galley, sat me at the table, and found the bottle of Powers Gold Label. She half-filled two tumblers and added a drop of water to each. I gulped mine. It lit me up from the inside and I started breathing more like a human being again and less like a fish. I looked at Paula. A pink glow was coming back to her cheeks.

"Next year," I said, "let's go camping." She was staring at me.

"You were marvelous," she said, generously.

I took her hand. "Marry me," I said.

And so she did. The following summer we went sailing, not camping. And eventually we took courage in hand and bought our own yacht and named her 'Sanctuary'.

Twenty years later and I'm not any braver than I was then. I dread bad weather. But I do know that come hell or high water, Paula and I, together, will face down any storm.

Tight Lines

ADAM TRODD, DUBLIN

Rain ran in swathes down the windscreen, the wipers swished back and forth at top speed. The visibility was so poor he nearly missed his exit off the motorway. A long promised fishing trip was the reason for his journey. With work piling up and clients to see every other day he didn't get a chance to name a date until his dad rang and said: "This Saturday. It's now or never. Those trout won't catch themselves."

By early evening the rain had cleared and the wet country roads were lined with bloom-laden blackthorn. He rolled down the window and breathed it all in. The gloom of the city receded as he pulled in through the gate. A warm hug at the front door while his collie, Jess, circled around their legs, tail wagging, told him he was home.

His dad got into his waders and jacket eagerly, and he could see how much the trip meant to him. The creak of the wicker fishing creel brought a smile to his face as he remembered catching minnows with his brother while their dad waded through the water in the distance, his line rhythmically whipping through the air.

His own gear was laid out in his old room. The scuffed little wallet of fishing flies and the smell of the wax jacket filled him with the old expectation of catching a trout. It was a short walk to the river through fields of yellow gorse and lark song.

"How's work?"

"Suddenly doesn't seem so important today, Dad." He put his hand down instinctively for Jess and tousled her ears.

On the bank, he watched his dad tie a fly to the line while a kingfisher flew upriver like a sapphire dart.

"You go on ahead, I'll follow," he said.

"I'm still trying to figure out what fly to use," I answered.

"Trying to figure out what your old man is using more like!"

The water sloshed and swirled around his waders as they strove against the lazy current. It wasn't long before he heard his dad's reel zip. The line lifted sharply from the water in a shower of droplets and a trout leapt high and shining in the late evening sun.

"One nil!" he shouted over.

Several fish later, they kitted up on the bank and chatted. "Will we swing by the village for one on the way home?"

"No need," his dad said, smiling. He lifted the lid of his creel to reveal two glasses and a bottle of Powers Gold Label. They sat on a wooden gate and savoured the chance to chat. "What took you so long, Son?"

Sins of Omission

PETER SOMERVILLE-LARGE, CARLOW

"It's Mooney," said the colonel's wife, replacing the receiver. "Someone to see the house. Someone important, he wouldn't say."

The colonel wasn't impressed. Since they had put the place up for sale they had been plagued by many useless and inquisitive buyers tramping through the rooms. He suspected several family objects had been pilfered.

An hour later the estate agent drove up. Then a small black Citroen could be seen bumping along the avenue towards the colonnaded porch. The dogs barked furiously as a smart chauffeur opened the back door and out stepped a tall clerical figure in black with a gold cross hanging from his neck.

"Oh my God." Who could fail to recognize that saturnine inquisitorial expression and those brooding eyes?

The dogs wagged their tails while the colonel and his wife shook hands briefly with the newcomer. They left it to the cringing estate agent to show him around.

"Should we invite him for tea?" There were the remains of a jam roll and Mary could make cucumber sandwiches, his wife said.

"That won't be necessary."

The inspection of the house did not take long, considering there were 18 bedrooms to view.

When they came out of the study, the colonel and his wife were surprised to see the two maids and the cook assembled in the great hall. As the cleric descended the main staircase they knelt. He held out his hand and on one of his long bony fingers was a ring which each of the servants brushed with a fleeting kiss.

He was affable when they said their farewells. They retired to the drawing room for a stiff glass of Powers Gold Label. "I have a feeling he is really interested in buying."

When they peered out of the long window, he was still there and the men who worked on the estate, some panting with the exertion of running, had gathered to pay him homage.

The cleric said nothing when he returned to the car, but he was pleased with his visit. Although in bad repair, the house was adequate for the purpose he had in mind. A chapel could be built in the corner of the ballroom and with a few concrete additions, there would be plenty of room for the order of missionaries who needed accommodation. He thought of the changes that would be made, the hunting prints, the lines of stuffed animal heads and the portrait of King William on his horse replaced by suitable devotional pictures. It was the first time the chauffeur had heard the archbishop laugh.

Whatever You're Having Yourself

YVONNE HALL, DUBLIN

Séan looked up from the bar when he heard the front door of the pub creak slowly open. A beam of light flashed on the wooden floor and nearly blinded him. It was still early on a Sunday afternoon and his head still throbbed from work the night before. He moved his cloth slowly across the counter, cursing the unexpected arrival. Then he saw her. A tall slim woman, with long brown hair, brown eyes and dark complexion seemed to appear out of the dazzling light. She was stunning. She wore a dark green coat with a red scarf around her neck. She was not from around here, that's for sure.

"Howya," was all he could manage.

At this stage she had passed by his bucket and mop and several tables stacked with chairs and was standing within a foot of him. He leaned on the counter for support. The lads wouldn't believe him, he thought. "All in your head," they'd say, "Stay clear of the mushrooms."

He had never seen anyone as beautiful, ever.

"What can I get ya?" he mumbled, mindful of his mother's 'oft repeated advice: "Don't gape son and close your mouth, or a wasp will fly in."

"Est ye thayer west? Sha edgepl elk," the visitor said in quiet calm voice, smiling expectantly.

Séan stared goggle-eyed at her. Was she having him on? Since there was no-one else around he decided to chance his arm.

"An bhfuil cúpla focal as Gaeilge agat?"

"Sedf resk jird isles," she answered, in the same, even voice.

"Ceart go leor," Séan replied, with an excessive flourish.

Séan eyed his bucket-full of hot water and detergent and thought about how, in the wink of an eye, his day had taken an almighty turn. "You can't really plan for the bad or the good or the great days," his father once said. "They just come upon you."

"Uisce beatha?" Séan said turning to the rows of bottles of liquor behind him.

"Essk ," came the reply.

So that was settled then. Séan pulled over the bottle of Powers Gold Label and set two glasses on the counter. Just to make sure he was on the right track, he gave her a sideways glance and raised the bottle. She smiled, nodded, and settled onto the bar stool. The conversation, such as it was, continued on its merry way.

Old Friends

PADRAIG DOYLE, DUBLIN

The Sweetman Cup, donated by Dr Noel Sweetman, the local GP, stood shiny, proud and battered on the bar of The Howling Nun. Where that name came from is another story altogether.

Peter and Mick had turned up like they had for the past eighteen years to try their luck in the annual trout fishing competition on the River Gartan. They had picked number eight in the draw for beats – the same one they picked three years previously when they came third by half an ounce.

No lines were allowed in the water before 9.30am, so they took their time driving to the river – less than a mile away. They paused briefly to survey the water, held a wet finger in the air to check the wind and nodded to each in silence as if to say "Could be good". They assembled their rods, squeaked into their knee boots and headed down the riverbank.

Reaching Beat Eight, they opened their fly boxes and were confronted by the usual mix of doubt, gut feeling and bravado. The more popular flies always looked well on the Gartan, but Peter had recently tied his own design – a grey, hairy pattern he called The Ronnie Drew, despite neither he nor Mick being Dubliners.

As expected, the river was fishing nicely. Both had their share of excitement – tugs which signaled either a fish or a rock – but geology was winning every time.

Around one o'clock, their plastic lunch-boxes and the coffee flasks were opened, almost in sync. Ham sandwiches for Mick, beef for Peter. They had seen splashes both upstream and downstream of them – and landing nets being stretched into the water to secure the catch – so they hoped the afternoon would bring them a catch. They flicked the cold dregs of their mugs into the hedge behind them, rose to their feet, and started casting again. Skill and experience were on their side, they said; they changed flies, tried shorter casts, longer casts, slowed-up the drift of the flu and speeded it up. It was just a question of being in the right place at the right time, they knew. All lines had to be out of the water by 5pm. Club helpers with binoculars saw to it that there was no cheating.

Back in The Howling Nun, Peter and Mick sat opposite each other and agreed it was another lovely day's fishing. They clicked their glasses of Powers with a smile. "To the driest landing net on the Gartan," said Mick. They both chuckled and knew the fish would be jumping again next year.

A Chance Encounter

BRIAN O'CONNOR, KERRY

We were too late. The seagulls wheeled and cried in the wake of the ferry as it pulled away from the dock, picked up speed and headed out into the estuary. No worries. My brother and I were just starting on a month-long cycling holiday around Ireland, and the golden red sunset held promise of another glorious autumn day to follow. What more could we ask for?

A girl's voice cut through the evening air. "It can't be the last ferry! God damn it, it's only eight thirty!"

There were three people standing on the pier; two very annoyed American girls by the sounds of it, their bikes lying on the ground, in full cycling gear like ourselves, hands on hips, facing down a man in a luminous yellow jacket.

"I'm sorry, ladies. Our winter schedule started last week. The last ferry leaves at half eight, except on Saturdays. The next one will be at nine tomorrow morning."

We free-wheeled down to the pier. The tallest girl turned to face us, pulled off her cycling helmet, and angrily shook out her long dark hair. "Can we do anything to help?" I offered, realising as I said it that it was a particularly stupid question, given the circumstances. "I doubt it, unless your bike floats."

Fair play, I had to admit.

"No," I said. "It doesn't do that."

The man in the jacket intervened. "The only place to stay overnight around here is over Nelligan's bar, just around the corner. I'll explain to Mary Nelligan what's happened. That's all I can do."

Once we'd changed, we headed straight downstairs to the pub, drawn by the smell of a turf fire and sounds of laughter. The Americans got in just before us. "Listen to me for once," my brother whispered, "this time let me do the talking." I nodded but when we reached them, I blurted out: "You two look different with your clothes on."

The only sound that broke the silence that followed was a low groan from my brother. Then the dark-haired girl smiled. "Mister," she said, "I'm sure you're a talented guy in some ways, but it ain't in one-liners. So, what are you good at?"

"Well," I said lamely, "I guess I'm good for buying you drink."

She snorted. "OK. What do you suggest here?"

"Nice pub, turf fire, good company and exacting conversation - it has to be Powers Gold Label whiskey."

And that's how I met Suzie. I asked her to marry me three times before she finally accepted. The first time was by text – that was a mistake. The second was after a fight. The third time? Well, that was a calculated, well-rehearsed effort in a carefully chosen restaurant in Dingle, over two glasses of Powers. What's not to love?

Short Pants

MARY CALLAGHAN, CORK

June was at its best, the sun splitting the rocks and swelling the hedgerows along the country roads. Most people would be at the beach, but Shay had only one thing on his mind: that this could be his year. He threw himself and his bicycle into the race with gusto.

He was well off the lead as he hit the last hill, but that didn't matter; Shay knew there was only one man to beat. Then out of the corner of his eye he saw Tom's front wheel edging up beside him. He barely had breath to mutter the words he'd shouted so many times in their childhoods and later in the family bakery business: "You'll not beat me, Short Pants!"

The finish line was only metres away. His legs felt as if they might explode but try as he might, Tom sprinted past him just at the line. Bragging rights to the little brother for another year, so.

Back at the house Mary was philosophical, as always. "It's only a charity cycle," she said. "I don't know why you two take these things so seriously. I'm only happy you didn't end up in the ditch." She gave him a kiss and opened the kitchen press where she kept the Powers Gold Label, handing him the bottle and two glasses. "Go on inside and put your feet up, he'll be here in a minute."

Shay was still nurturing the sting of defeat when the doorbell rang. It was Tom and Annette.

"Come to gloat, have you?" he asked, standing up with a grimace.

Tom's big laugh filled the room as he threw an arm around his brother. "Sure you know I have, aul fella!" he said. "It's seldom enough I get the chance, you have to admit." He spotted the bottle on the table. "Ah, good stuff, you didn't forget. To the victor come the spoils, so!"

Their wives left them to it.

Shay poured Tom a Powers and topped up his own. "Well, the best man won, as Dad would've said."

Tom raised his glass. "To next year," he said, "and another chance to beat you."

They went silent for a moment, steeped in memories. It was Shay who spoke first. "Jaysus, I'm banjaxed," he said, and they laughed like drains, like they were boys again.

What Maisie Did

ANDREA CARTER, DUBLIN

Maisie pressed her powdered cheek against the cool glass and closed her eyes. The raucous chanting from the back of the bus seemed a million miles way as she drifted off to sleep with her coat wrapped around her shoulders. She awoke just as they were approaching the outskirts of the city and came to as she always did with a gradual feeling of anxiety until she remembered where she was. She hugged herself with inward glee.

She wondered what the busload of supporters she had joined in Ennis thought of the little white-haired, seventy-year-old travelling on her own in her funny old clothes. Truth be told they probably hadn't given her a second glance. If the bus went on fire now and the survivors had to identify the missing passengers, she'd bet no one would remember her. That was what happened when you got old, you became invisible to anyone younger, and as time went on that meant more and more people just couldn't see you at all.

But Frank could see her. Frank had always been able to see her, since that first time with wild flowers in her hair at that music festival in 1961. Could that really be fifty years ago? When did they get so old?

She shook herself. Enough of those thoughts. It was because of Frank she was here, on her way to the All-Ireland. He couldn't bear the idea of not being able to see Clare play in Croke Park after all this time and she was to go, and tell him all about it.

The bus finally ground to a halt and the crowd filed off, scarves and banners waving, still singing. Maisie got off with them and joined the queue to get into the park.

Up in the stands her mind continued its meandering as the crowd around her grew more and more excited. Clare scored. The fans went wild. Maisie rose from her seat. She pushed her way along the crowded row to the edge of the stand and made her way slowly down towards the pitch.

Sitting up in bed Frank took a sip from his glass and punched the air in delight. They were going to win. He could feel it in his bones. Suddenly something in the bottom left hand corner of the television screen distracted him from the play. The crowd had started to cheer again. Clearly visible, skipping gleefully across the pitch and waving a Clare flag was Maisie, white hair bobbing. Stark naked.

A delighted smile crept across his face. He raised his glass of Powers Gold Label at the screen.

"That's the spirit Maisie. That's my girl."

Positive Equity

NEIL BURKEY, LONDON

I'd been digging for more than an hour. My hands were already blistered and my back was aching – the ground was full of stones and this was unaccustomed work for me. "You really think this is going to work?" I shouted, but got no response. I stuck the shovel in the mound of earth and sat down, my feet hovering above the hole. It was warm for early April and I had worked up a mighty sweat. I dragged my sleeve across my forehead somewhat dramatically and looked once more at the instruction sheet that had come with the kit.

"How to bury St Joseph: Pick a prime spot in the garden of the house you wish to sell and dig a hole deep enough to fit your Sell Your Home Quick St Joseph statue. Place the statue upside-down in the hole and cover him up. Say your prayers and within four weeks you will find your buyer!"

I threw the instructions over my shoulder and scratched my head. St Joseph stood next to me in a robe, holding his big staff and giving me a slightly quizzical look.

"Sorry about this, Joe," I said, and after shooting a look at the house I picked him up and stuck him face-first in the soil. But despite my efforts, his little feet were still poking up above the ground. I considered trying to tamp him down with the shovel but it just didn't seem right considering what we were asking him to do for us. I sighed and closed my eyes for a moment. When I opened them, I saw a second pair of feet; they were attached to my wife.

"Going well then, is it?" she said.

She sat down beside me bearing a tray with two tumblers half-filled with whiskey. "I've poured you a Powers," she said. "I thought you might need some. I thought I might need some too."

"What are we going to do about those feet?" I asked.

"What indeed."

Just then the sun broke through the clouds and bathed the house in a warm glow. The clematis overhanging the portcullis danced lightly in the breeze and a clutch of goldfinches lit upon the lawn. We drank and watched as they picked apart the thistles.

"Well," she said, while the whiskey burned pleasantly in my throat, "maybe it's not such a bad house after all."

"Yeah, maybe not," I said, "maybe not." She put her arm around my shoulder and gave me a little squeeze. "And what should we do about Joseph?" I asked.

She took a sip from her glass and looked at the house. "Bury him anyway."

Kindred Spirits

GINA MACMAHON, KILDARE

They were home on holidays from London. "Next stop the country cousins!" Gareth laughed as we drove down the bumpy boreen. The farmhouse was old and expansive, as was the welcome. We sat down for tea and warm scones when an order, disguised as an invitation, came from on high. "Send up Gerry's son's intended wife!"

The room was old-fashioned but bright, a lemon candlewick bedspread adorning the brass bed, flowery curtains framing the open window. "Who have I here?" Aunt Minnie asked imperiously from the bed.

"This is Sarah," Gareth said, bending to kiss her. She dismissed him. "You give a hand with the cows, we'll have a little chat," she said. It sounded ominous. "Sit down, girl," she gestured. "Tell me, what do you do with yourself?"

"I'm a marketing consultant," I said, smiling broadly to soften the blow.

"Not a nurse or teacher then?"

"No," I answered as pleasingly as I could, "but I still have time."

"Not that much time," she sniffed, "you won't be turned back at the altar anyway."

"Sure I mightn't turn up at all," I countered.

"What a fool you'd be," she scoffed, smoothing down her bedcovers, "with the big farm of land coming at you."

The architect I was marrying had never mentioned a farm, but I hid my surprise.

"Well," I jollied along, "we'll just have to wait and see."

"I doubt," she went on, "you'd be much use on a farm anyway."

I gave it my best shot. "Maybe not, but I could probably manage to stand in a gap if he was herding cows."

She liked that. "You mightn't be as green as you look," she smirked. "Will you have a small one with me?"

I knew the small one wasn't an espresso. I had already spotted the side table laden with a well-worn silver tray and a beckoning bottle of Powers Gold Label nestled among the good tumblers. I moved to the table.

"You'll be wanting something fancy in it?" she provoked.

I didn't bite. "No, I like it just as it comes."

"It seems," she said slowly, "we both like our whiskey the way I always liked my men."

I glanced at her, at her mischievous eyes. "You mean straight?" I asked incredulously.

"Well, that was usually a given dear," she said. "I was actually going to say, neat."

Thoroughly Modern Grandmother

MAEVE BANCROFT, CORK

I'm perhaps happiest when milking my cow and enjoy resting my forehead against her rump. It's warm and I can hear her chewing contentedly. It's a lovely sound, as is the sound of the milk squirting into the bucket. People are sometimes taken aback when they hear "cow" rather than "herd" and "bucket" rather than "machine", but I've handed over the farm to my only child and he has the herd and machines to contend with and I have my cow. We're both getting on in years but neither of us will be sent to the slaughterhouse. Yet.

I love Thursdays as it's the night of my weekly date. After the milking I do a few jobs around the place and then I tart myself up; it's important to make an effort and look half-way decent. I take my favourite bottle out of the cupboard and add a drop of cold water to my glass while I settle down in front of my laptop, a present from my grand-daughter, so we can Skype each other. She lives in New York and is lactose intolerant, which coming from a dairy farm is kind of funny. Anyway, whenever anyone goes over to visit her I send a Baby Powers as a reminder of good times at home with a note saying not to drink too much and to say her prayers, neither of which she heeds, probably.

For her 30th birthday, I'm sending her a pair of Manolos, something her generation loves by all accounts. I went to the local shoe shop where they had a great laugh telling me that I'd have to travel to Cork to buy such flashy shoes. As the bit was between my teeth I headed straight up. I wasn't their usual type of customer. When I mentioned they were for my one and only glamorous grand-daughter they couldn't do enough to help, including providing a phone so I could get on to her mother as I'd forgotten to get her shoe size.

The wrapping was extensive and the bill expensive and they even offered to send it to her but there was another gift to go with the shoes - a celebratory little bottle of Powers. I went to a nearby pub to buy one (and a drink for myself as I wasn't over the shock of the price of the shoes) and as I sat and relaxed I laughed to myself at the realisation that the shoes cost the same as my cow. We'll both have a good laugh at that when she gets the shoes, and we meet again on Skype.

Clear Water Revival

CLARE O'BRIEN-MORAN, WESTMEATH

"What glorious weather for April and so few people around to enjoy it." The old man didn't move as I appeared. His profile was all I could see and his weathered features could have been carved from stone. He made no effort to turn in my direction but continued staring in his meditative state.

"Grand day," I said. "T'is, thank God," he replied without wavering his gaze from the horizon.

"How is it?" I asked.

"Lovely," was his short answer. I put my towel down on a rock and began to undress. Each layer that I removed released the trapped heat from my body. The sun wasn't as warm here and with the sea breeze, goose pimples were rising all over my skin. I stood on the edge of the pier and considered the sea below. It must certainly be several degrees colder here than it had been at the car, but its glistening surface rose and fell, calling me like a siren.

I poised, prayed, and dived straight in. Arrgh! My brain was screaming Arrgh! The freezing water swirled above me as I tried to surface and catch my breath. Its icy pull enveloped me. Panic paralyzed my arms and legs. Was I mad? I forced myself to swim a few strokes out to sea, then turned and paddled back. As I climbed up the ladder, the old devil sat there grinning.

"Fresh, isn't it?" he said.

I grabbed my towel and rubbed my skin with its rough surface, as though I could erase the freezing sensation that seemed to have now reached my bones.

"Gosh, Dad, you might have warned me!"

"Since when did you start listening to me? You always had to find out for yourself."

"I could have had a heart attack!"

"Don't be so dramatic, sure don't I go in every day and I'm still alive. Here, have a sip," he said, passing me the cup from his flask.

"Tea?" I enquired innocently.

"Pah! It's a full measure of Powers. It'll revive you."

We sat on our towels in silence, watching the rise and swell of the water. An occasional gull swooped by and called, while its companions bobbed about on the sea.

"Aren't you having some?"

"Sure there's only one cup and you look like you need it more than I do."

"Sláinte," I said. The whiskey warmed my chattering lips before slipping smoothly down my throat.

"Don't tell your mother," he replied.

New Perspectives

LAUREN CROTHERS, DUBLIN

The tears seeped, hot and wet, into the grey cardigan on her mother's shoulder. She felt she'd never let go, but knew it was coming, standing there like two entwined statues in a whirlwind. The activity was picking up all around them and finally the voices on the tannoy became unbearable. She walked away, got on that flight and left. Left family, friends, the rain-sodden dole queue, the green, grey and flashes of gold. One of millions, past and present, a thread in a blanket so huge it covers the world.

But despite the pining for home and the lingering doubt, here was this new life, in a country both beguiling and menacing, trying to find its feet again after war and genocide. She struggled to take it all in: a barefoot monk in brilliant saffron waiting silently for his alms; a family of four astride a little battered motorbike; an overcrowded hospital ward creaking under the weight of a mass tragedy. The surprising yet gentle touch of a child's fingers connecting the freckled dots on her arm. And all the while, amid this carousel of colour and grime and innate kindness, that little pang for the familiar.

It was to be found in a dusty, faded side street behind the soaring steeple of a pagoda, past the sweet and sour aroma emanating from street food stalls and the clatter of chopsticks against plastic bowls. She found a little bar, with various knick-knacks fighting for space on the smoke-stained walls. She sat and eyed the bottles, some in need of a shine, and suddenly, she grinned. She'd come all this way to the land of the unfamiliar, to what she thought was a seemingly backwater bar, and there was a bottle of Powers Gold Label on the shelf. "One of those," she said in the language that was becoming easier for her. Just then her phone beeped with a message from home, a reminder that today's emigrants are never too far away from what they may be missing.

So she sat holding the glass and considered her plight. Thought of all those out there who had left, under duress or not, to flee or to seek. She decided she was a seeker and that, despite the challenges she'd experienced and the ones that lay ahead, it was ok to look back, but not to give up on this new place - replete with trauma and triumph - just yet. And she knew, whether her future lay back among the green and grey or here, among the blushes of orange and pink, there would still be those flashes of gold. And that all would be well.

The Powers of Dreams

JANE BURNS, MEATH

Like many of my generation, I left Ireland in the 1980s hoping for a chance at a future, some payback for my parents' sacrifice to send me to university. They were proud when I graduated, the first one ever in our family, but their pride was tinged with sadness as they knew I would have to go away to earn a living and make a life for myself.

My father, a man of few words, handed me an envelope with €500 in it and said: "Son, take care and call your mother every Sunday." Mam, well, she just cried and put a jar of homemade jam in my rucksack and hugged me.

Every Sunday I would call. Da would answer and the conversation never changed. "How's the weather?", "Do you need money?", "When you come home, get me some Powers in the duty- free."

Things were going well. I was able to come home more and more often and each time Da would pick me up at the airport. I would deliver, as promised, the Powers, and his eyes would light up when we got home as he'd pour us both a short one.

Eventually I met the woman of my dreams. We moved back home to Ireland and got married. I got a great job that took me around the world and anytime I went away, on the way back I'd always get the Powers. Even though I could have claimed the taxi on expenses, Da always picked me up. We used to joke it was for the Powers and not to see me.